Retrofuturism f

Oz Hardwick

First published 2024 by The Hedgehog Poetry Press

Published in the UK by
The Hedgehog Poetry Press
Coppack House, 5
Churchill Avenue
Clevedon
BS21 6QW

www.hedgehogpress.co.uk

ISBN: 978-1-916830-17-2

9 8 7 6 5 4 3 2 1

A CIP Catalogue record for this book is available from the British
Library.

Contents

Boys! Build Your Own Time Machine!

Choose your wood carefully: the harder the better. Oak may be the most obvious, but you may consider elm for its connotations of new beginnings, or even the beech to invoke the aid of the divine feminine. Don't just settle on the easiest option, and don't be ashamed if it asks you about your desires. Pay particular attention to scent: is it closer to an empty corridor that echoes with the sound of chairs scraping on floorboards and a voice as monotonous as a stopped clock, or to the sting of brambles on your berry-stained hand? Then, listen to its stories, noting fluctuations in angles of incidence and refraction, and variations in volume and temperature. Count its rings and plot intersections with medullary rays: these figures will not be procedurally necessary, but may foster an illusion of stability and control which has been found comforting in ±86% of reported cases. Switch off all artificial light sources – not forgetting standby indicators and hand-held devices – and, as each is extinguished, call to mind gentle arms, a radio turned low, and the smell of a winter coat. Now, build your time machine.

Democracy: An Evolutionary Perspective

We came down from the trees on the back of a slim majority, blinded by convincing projections of a temperate climate and a short commute to the career of our choice, and by dazzling promises of comfortable footwear and a mouth-watering selection of nutritious ready-meals to be enjoyed within our nuclear family units. Not just TV, but the whole world, would be there to inform, educate, and entertain us, our glowing children, and their beautifully mutated offspring, catering to everyone's exponentially-evolving bodies and desires. A significant minority grumbled that no one was really sure what 'exponentially' actually meant, but they were pretty sure it was being used willy-nilly and, besides, our bodies were fine as they were, perfectly acclimatised to the arboreal overstory. But democracy's democracy, with all its shiny toys and distractions, and the public gets what the public generally doesn't want, from lo-salt sludge at dangerous temperatures, to the Big Red Button on rigged talent shows and the global nuclear stage. I live alone and fret about the weather, sharing my fears on the dark web with increasingly disgruntled AI. When the next election comes, I shall vote with my feet, discarding my shoes and carving a cross in the last remaining tree.

The Birth of Modern Britain

We lower the babies into paper boats, like our mothers did when we were just wriggly bits of flesh and wind. It's that one day of summer when the collective noun for mothers is a mumble, and the pond's a humming bumble, a hive with a hundred queens. Honey sticks like sunlight around pink, puckering lips which air-kiss the magic of *ooh* and *ah*. *Ooh* and *ah*. The babies are decked in their best family charms, their wrists wound in tiny bracelets, and their chests rising and falling like the very waves beneath jewel-encrusted beetles. The mothers are wrapped in bristling black and gold. Meanwhile, fire-blackened fathers loll in the shadows, reading important papers and clicking their tongues like thirsty birds. *Ooh* and *ah*: just look at all the boats! Look at the blur of all those mothers' wings! If I had a camera, I'd reel off picture after picture, but such inventions are way in the future.

Problems in Eschatological Cartography

The West Pier creaked and belly-flopped into the wild, wild sea. This was not the *oh* we were expecting, not the *ah* we'd predicted. There were limp rafts flapping at the lip of the land, nostalgic seafarers standing and staring charismatically at the horizon. The world was green and grey, and the West Pier waved from the waves as it wallowed, swallowing the peril it had put off for generations. It was neither the crash of bankers nor the Fall of rebel angels. It was not the knotty conundrum with which we had wrestled when we should have been taking practical steps. Then, the West Pier disappeared from view, leaving nothing but uneven steps into the grey-green problematic. There were reports on the local news, but the nationals had bigger fish to fry, as the sky fried and the bigger fish stepped onto land.

The Trip of a Lifetime

Another day, another billionaire strokes the tail of space, slips away from belted gravity, and floats like the embryo of a new species that has no reason to exist. Flight without feathers, flight without wings, flight without responsibility, running a rippling trail across new mountains. A glance of zig-zag light. White horizon. Harp seals roll in twenty-four-hour sun, and a silver sliver slides on shrinking ice. Money talks of twisting in zero-G but, just as the song says, it can't buy love. It can't buy more than six or seven minutes of evolution. It can't buy exemption from burning up on landing.

Process of Illumination

One year the roof fell in without warning. One minute it was there, doing roof things, holding up birds and stars, and keeping us in our safe space. Hearth and home. And then it was at our ankles, its fragments snapping like crabs at low tide, leaving us to lift like balloons into places we'd previously only known through metaphors. Fields and palaces. The miracle was that no one was hurt. Hundreds died and who knows how many – thousands? millions? – vanished without trace. But no one was hurt, no one felt anything other than abstract nouns: mostly ambivalence but also mild curiosity. Nothing so mundane as weight, or as prosaic as hope. You'd think there would have been a period of adjustment, and of debate leading to a new dispensation, but we were marble statues in a field of light. We were waves rolling in across a golden shore.

Reflections on the Perpetual Motion Machine

The small machine is made of walls, like a maze for mice, or a labyrinth for light as it dodges through prisms and mirrors. Its function is unclear, though it carries many implications, a synecdoche for the city which never weeps as it rolls into its unplanned future. It's too big for my pocket, too awkward for my hand, too fragile to jostle in a rucksack, and too valuable to leave at home as I go about my daily tasks. So, I shuffle simulations beneath the skin of the machine, where white walls stretch on and on to fine bright suburbs and the promise of realistic weather. And the machine sings: it sings like a beehived diva with a breaking heart and quivering lips, mascara smudged and shoes kicked off in angsty backstage fug; it sings like a fresh-faced speed-eyed mop-top, sweat glistening under scorching tungsten; it sings like a whisky-sanded piano man in the rattle of gunfire and squealing tyres. Maybe this is what it was made for, though I love it best when it's silent, when the walls line up like ivory dominoes, and when I can barely risk breathing lest I compromise its intricate beauty.

Etiquette in the Age of Deserts

Now that the water is disappearing, we're careful not to spill. Remember those Pathé newsreels of debutantes with books balanced on their heads, their spines straight as answers to tough questions? It's like that. Remember sheer silk on shoulders the colour and temperature of fresh milk, rippling with the light of assumed privilege? It's like that. Remember that clipped voice with arched eyebrows and its little finger crooked around a dimpled tumbler? It's like all that, but dryer and more fearful. What no one remembers, though, is what those books were. If asked, eight out of ten of us would probably assume it was Debrett's, with the rest split between encyclopaedias, dictionaries, or maybe something by Shakespeare. Truth to tell, they were bound copies of Svante Arrhenius's 1896 paper warning of the climate impact of changes in atmospheric CO_2 levels. Maybe, just maybe, instead of mooning over those pretty, interchangeable faces, and smiling at the voiceover's witty *bon mot*, we should have read the warnings. Remember when everything was black, white, and inevitable? It's like that.

In an Absence of Birds

Today's sky is a tapestry, threaded with all the things we've thrown at clouds which never came down. The warp and weft of balloons and curses is a field of forgotten losses: bottle rockets, dolls suspended from tissue parachutes, a million paper planes, and all those fabled apples tossed back into trees. Vapour trails thread lines and letters, streaming phylacteries of commentary, exegesis, and the words of homely wisdom our grandmothers shared over steaming tea. It's all so low that I can feel its coarse nap on my sunburnt shoulders, and I'm sure that, if I can just catch that dangling thread, I can unravel the whole world and start again. Tomorrow's sky may well be a net of beached fish or a nest of vines and vipers. After that, it's anybody's guess. A drifting doll at the Kármán Line surveys embroidered Earth, bites into a golden apple, and assesses what exactly may be saved by a stitch or two, in or out of time.

Storm Forecast

This is the room where radio waves bleed, as if the air was cracked skin. Osmosis and semi-permeable membranes, and all those things we remember from school which are shorn of meaning after all this time. Angles of incidence, radii of circles. The function of x within complex equations or at the bottom of a note passed in class. The waves are maybe tidal, maybe threatening erosion of seemingly solid surfaces, and maybe need a Band-Aid. This is the emergency room, the panic room, the room for improvement at the end of a dark school corridor, where skin cracked as loving mothers waved goodbye. I turn off the radio, but the waves keep crashing across absorbent wallpaper and I'm soaked to my broken skin. If a boat leaves the harbour travelling at 18 knots in a south-westerly direction, how long will it take to fall off the edge of the world? The room is locked and the radio is nothing but water. My hands are cracked waves. There are ten minutes remaining before every one of us must put down our pens and staunch the bleeding.

The Last Outpost

Outside, the flower of our muddy uniforms blooms beneath cackling selves. It's just another war zone, with skin as far as we care to consider. There's no time out there, no space in here, and we've coined the word *neverything* to describe all the details. There are two suns, though even they are hardly enough to illuminate the fractures. I can still see the circus, mirrored in windows; still feel the curses, mired in wind. Neverything occurs simultaneously and, like our uniforms, we are hung out to dry in the two suns. Static plants crackle. Planes crack. It's just another drop zone, its skin stripped bare, and I can still hear the cries of widows.

Landmarks in Interstellar Travel

The harder we push, the further we drift: the sharper we touch, the louder we forget. It's a workable hypothesis that time is skin, or that hearts can be measured in light years; and though scientists balk at the term 'solar system,' there's no denying we've left something behind, and that it's becoming colder as echoes stretch so far apart that they lose their own voices. As gravity decreases, so blame melts: as words freeze, blood boils. It's more nurture than nature, but I used to collect bubblegum cards of moments like this, with anonymous suits reflecting stars at the end of a thin cord, and I imagine swapping doubles of today for something I've never seen. There are instruments for measuring the mass of your hair, the radiation of your lips, and the escape velocity of every syllable that lights up the pre-dawn motorway. Most of the risk is in take-off or landing, but we can't stay forever pinned to blank charts, our memories cross-fading in the heartbeat of the only sun we can maybe trust.

Retrofuturism for the Dispossessed

Old enough to know better, but too poor to afford it, we make do and mend, while scissoring pictures from shiny magazines to slip beneath our pillows and redirect our dreams. I dream of drawing down the Moon on a fine thread until it's so close that I can step across into the better future we were promised on TV. I call out to my whole family, and we ride a gleaming rail to a crystal city that grows from grey sand into a song of pulsing colour. A robot dog welcomes us to our new home, and we dine on the best supermarket brands, heated to perfection, in front of a 3D TV that fills the living room wall. Dad lets me try his small cigar and I cough and cough until I cry with laughter. Outside the window, the Earth slips away. When we wake up, you tell me you dreamed of walking forever on a road suspended above the sea, with gas lamps sparking on to light the way as night fell. Your feet were frozen from the undulating waves. I show you the grey sand on my slippers, the ash down the front of my dressing gown. *It'll get better*, you tell me.

Halcyon

No one expects wings, yet they come to us all sooner or later. The old soldier waiting at the bus stop, the young boy threading daisies in the field beyond the town. The blue-black bird may appear as a speck in the sky, which we'll watch with curiosity as it draws closer, growing beyond reason. Or maybe we'll be otherwise absorbed, lost in thoughts of all the things we could have, should have, said or done when those rare chances flashed by: and we'll snap from reverie at the subtle *shush* of feather against feather, and look into kind, hard eyes. Either way, we'll stagger slightly with the weight of phantom limbs made manifest, slap and flap like waking babies. The blue-black bird will bob and hop, stretching its span to the limit of imagination, then just that little bit further. It's important to be ready for this inevitable gift: it's important to understand that we won't be.

Negotiable

Tomorrow, I downloaded the timEbay app, where you could bid for better pasts and futures. That's *app*, as in appetite, and the apple that really, really should have remained unbitten: tasty but trouble. Apprehension in its multiple meanings. Appease my palpitating heart and touch the sensitive screen. When I was a buoy, I bobbed in a limitless ocean; now, I'm my own amanuensis, taking down my own misfingered notes. Parp parp! Appalling! Awkward appendages appear disjointed, but I press *Approve*, and proceed. Time, it seems, is saleably unstable, with all its appropriate appurtenances infinitely variable for the right price. I place a small and perfectly formed fortune I may never have known upon the roll of bones, to the approbation and applause of appointed authorities. Apprised of my rights, I down my load in disrupted waves. We will be able to bid for better futures and presents. Now is a gift appended to all well-appointed applications. Appreciate this moment. Now this one. Can you tell the difference? There's an app for that.

Not as Advertised

When it eventually arrived, I'd expected the future to be different: but there it was, overpacked and obvious where it had been left by the delivery driver. The name and address were smudged by drizzle, and the damp cardboard clearly hadn't been handled with care. I manoeuvred it inside – it was awkwardly large, though it hardly weighed a thing – but I needed the bathroom, so I left it in the hall and went upstairs. I was only a few minutes, but when I came down the box had gone, and it wasn't my house. In fact, it wasn't a house at all, but a florist's shop, with water streaming down the inside of the plate glass window in a way that I hadn't seen for decades. I chose a bunch of snowdrops gripped by a tight blue band and, as there was nobody to take it, left the exact money on the counter. Outside the shop, I found my own front steps, with a delivery driver holding out a parcel, asking me to sign for it and pay an excess postage charge. I couldn't remember my name, so signed yours instead, and I had no change, so I gave him the snowdrops. The parcel was smaller than I'd expected, but so close that it looked huge.

Acknowledgments

'Boys! Build Your Own Time Machine!' was published as part of Silver Birch Press's *How To* series (8 March 2021). 'The Trip of a Lifetime' was published in *International Times* (8 July 2023).

There's a hackneyed old adage that says write what you know. What I know better than anything is entropy, uncertainty, and lurching shifts in temporal perception, and I have come to realise that this might well be what I've always written, regardless of style or ostensible subject. It seems appropriate, then, to offer thanks to the artists in diverse media who, long before I was even consciously paying attention, first showed me that such sensations could be alchemised into something beautiful – even it that beauty itself could sometimes be grotesque or even terrifying. And I'm immensely grateful to two of them for their generous words on this slim collection. If you don't know them, I urge you to check out Michael Butterworth's collected short fiction, *Butterworth* (Null23, 2019), and Arthur Brown's most recent album, *Long Long Road* (Prophecy/Magnetic, 2022).

"Reading this poetry is like walking in the countryside and coming upon a wood. It looks dense and solid and, in places where the bushes greet you at the tree line, impenetrable. As you step into them you may find nettles and thorns give you a foreboding welcome, but as you get in deeper, they thin out, and you are left with occasional thickets and moss and tree trunks.

Just as the patterns in the bush barriers were dense and intricately and haphazardly woven, the trees in the forest seem to have simpler, larger written, and bolder patterns.

It takes a full step into this poetry to appreciate fully the organic wholeness of its formation and to feel the underlying world it is creating, in which all the apparently separate organisms are made whole under the surface by being rooted in the fungi universe. In these poems the verses are separate aspects of one whole being's perspective – through the thoughts, revelations, impressions, questions and feelings expressed in the words of the poet.

Time dissolves before our very eyes as, with humour, Oz fearlessly dissects hopes, dreams, and delusions – science and nature come together and are unable to undo the human conundrum. Safe to say that if we observe ourselves and our history, and the history of our hopes and fears, at least humour can let us see our predicament and have a touchingly warm, if cynical, glance at ourselves."

– *Arthur Brown*

"This slim guide might be The Schoolboys' Rebellion because, as the writer laments, the future's not how the bubble-gum cards once described it.

Hardwick's haunting threnodies for the world reek with sorrow at the present age and return you to childhood when a time machine could still be built, and an imagined future was still possible.

In his textual steppingstones to once imagined futures and beleaguered pasts, billionaires vainly "stroke the tail of space" while the writer tries to stem Collapse. Already, meaning has fled and comforts have gone.

But the here and now is what counts, he seems to say, and when our eyes are taken off what really matters then evolution will find its own solution. His implied remedy is to walk a gentle path home into remembering what once was and to build renewal.

As with any Hardwick micro-fictions of recent years these will raise your vision to arrive at an unexpected view of human nature and a new appreciation of possibility."

– *Michael Butterworth*